RIDICULOUS LIGHT

THE LEXI RUDNITSKY FIRST BOOK PRIZE IN POETRY

The Lexi Rudnitsky First Book Prize in Poetry is a collaboration between Persea Books and The Lexi Rudnitsky Poetry Project. It sponsors the annual publication of a collection by a woman who has yet to publish a full-length poetry book.

Lexi Rudnitsky (1972–2005) grew up outside of Boston. She studied at Brown University and Columbia University, where she wrote poetry and cultivated a profound relationship with a lineage of women poets that extends from Muriel Rukeyser to Heather McHugh. Her own poems exhibit both a playful love of language and a fierce conscience. Her writing appeared in *The Antioch Review, Columbia: A Journal of Literature and Art, The Nation, The New Yorker, The Paris Review, Pequod*, and *The Western Humanities Review*. In 2004, she won the Milton Kessler Memorial Prize for Poetry from *Harpur Palate*. Lexi died suddenly in 2005, just months after the birth of her first child and the acceptance for publication of her first book of poems, *A Doorless Knocking into Night* (Mid-List Press, 2006). The Lexi Rudnitsky First Book Prize in Poetry was founded to memorialize her and to promote the type of poet and poetry in which she so spiritedly believed.

PREVIOUS WINNERS OF THE LEXI RUDNITSKY FIRST BOOK PRIZE IN POETRY

2017	Emily Van Kley	*The Cold and the Rust*
2016	Molly McCully Brown	*The Virginia State Colony for Epileptics and Feebleminded*
2015	Kimberly Grey	*The Opposite of Light*
2014	Susannah Nevison	*Teratology*
2013	Leslie Shinn	*Inside Spiders*
2012	Allison Seay	*To See the Queen*
2011	Laura Cronk	*Having Been an Accomplice*
2010	Cynthia Marie Hoffman	*Sightseer*
2009	Alexandra Teague	*Mortal Geography*
2008	Tara Bray	*Mistaken for Song*
2007	Anne Shaw	*Undertow*
2006	Alena Hairston	*The Logan Topographies*

RIDICULOUS
LIGHT
POEMS
VALENCIA
ROBIN

A KAREN & MICHAEL BRAZILLER BOOK
PERSEA BOOKS / NEW YORK

Persea Books, Inc.
90 Broad Street
New York, New York 10004

Library of Congress Cataloging-in-Publication Data
Names: Robin, Valencia, 1958– author.
Title: Ridiculous light : poems / Valencia Robin.
Description: New York : Persea Books, [2019] | "A Karen & Michael Braziller = Book."
Identifiers: LCCN 2018049882 | ISBN 9780892554966 (original trade pbk. : alk= . paper)
Classification: LCC PS3618.O317594 A6 2019 | DDC 811/.6—dc23
LC record available at https://lccn.loc.gov/2018049882

Book design and composition by Rita Lascaro
Typeset in Georgia
Manufactured in the United States of America. Printed on acid-free paper.

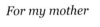

For my mother

CONTENTS

One

Two

Three

RIDICULOUS LIGHT

ONE

Cathedral

Not that I needed reminding, but even the trees, the trees!
Like giant awestruck afros grown in the laboratory
of a mad brother, the nerdy Nerudian of my dreams
who's somehow isolated the colors of all the saddest love songs

in the world—*Baby, baby red* and *Please, please, please
yellow*, yes, even the browns are talking to me, the greens
blue in this early autumn light that makes everything shout.
And where's my hopeless agnostic when I need her,

foreseer of endless wars and sorrows? Is that her running
toward that old abandoned church, cathedral of shadow
and grass? The leaves above trembling like tambourines,
two happy squirrels dancing down the aisle.

Dutch Elm Disease

When Danny Johnson's big brother was killed in Vietnam,
Danny ran around the block five times. I counted. Ran
as if when he stopped his brother would be back in their driveway
washing his car. But nobody knew anything about time travel
back then, *Star Trek* hadn't even come out, Lieutenant Uhura
still on Broadway doing *Blues for Mr. Charlie.* And even if Danny
did understand the space-time continuum, his parents
weren't having it, his mother on the porch yelling
his name, his father tackling him on the front lawn, all us kids,
the whole block standing there on pause. Which didn't exist
either. No fast forward, no reverse. We weren't even Black
yet. Was Milwaukee even Milwaukee? Is the Lincoln Park Bridge
still there, do boys like Danny still climb over the rail,
hug their bony knees to their narrow chests and plop into the river
as if there's no way his parents could lose *two* children?
Which is all I know about Vietnam, that and the way the sun hung
in the faded sky as Danny ran around and around
and held the air hostage, that and the way the thick August air
ignored the leaves of all our doomed elm trees
and let itself be held hostage. The streets were like ghosts
when they cut down those trees.

Kitchen Clock

Beware of my friend Jan's stories,
the one about her tour of the famous church
and the hysterical child, how the mother
had to practically carry the kid out,
the girl, seven or eight, screaming,
I want to see God! I want to see God!
See what I mean. Not that it wasn't slightly funny
before Jan explained it was the day after the school shootings.
Listen, I didn't even want to come to dinner,
had a bad cold, longed to be home in bed—but Jan was visiting,
my friend who was trying to change her life,
who'd quit her job, the dark room of her face lit for weeks
with this ridiculous light. Yes, beware of all that hope,
not to mention friends who move away, who tell stories
and then start crying which means you have to rub their backs
and think about those kids and their families
or imagine the little girl in the church, her face
all screwed up—and her mind, what about her mind?
Then I drive home and there are five deer
sitting on the snow in my backyard. And, yes, I know
they eat your tulips and your pansies, that there's
nothing otherworldly about them—the point is, I'm *city*
so five of anything and I'm backing up. No antlers
means they're female, right? One was chewing something,
otherwise they were just calmly watching
me, their eyes so sweet and dumb. And you know where this is
going, of course, how when I get cold and rush inside
and the deer all turn toward the window
even though I didn't turn on the light, that it's too late
to act as if my kitchen is just a kitchen
—and that cheap clock ticking too loudly
behind me, who'd think *that's* what I'd be holding on to
when I finally let go.

Milwaukee, 1968

Say it loud! I'm black and I'm proud
—James Brown

I was there the day *black* stopped
being the worst thing you could call somebody.
Right on 16th Street between Friebrantz
and Olive. The day before, the exact same word
could get you beat up or spanked, but that morning
we turned on the radio and it was as if the sun had come out
of the closet, as if the moon was burning her underwear.
And we didn't just stand around and watch
either. Me, Michael, Sherrie, David,
and Theresa—we marched up and down the street
singing ourselves into brand new people,
doing our part to free the nation.
And when the street lights came on, I marched
right up the stairs to our second floor flat
still singing *loud* and *proud*, praying my mother
had heard we weren't colored anymore, kind of worried
and yet no turning back, marching around
the kitchen table, was not going to be moved,
finally peeking over at my mother washing dishes,
spying her trying not to laugh
and wonder who I'd be if she'd done the opposite,
if by the following week we weren't both wearing afros.

Intermezzo

Can the thirsty stay sane after what they've seen?
—Phoebe Snow

Sometimes you hear a song,
like her song,
that fits like a ripe plum in your hand,
the sweet flesh and tart skin of her voice
—simply what it is.

Like tall grass gone to flower,
the simplest of yellows.
Or the right man opening
a jar and handing it back to you, smiling.
The jar holding something
you'd almost forgotten.

Geese

When your father isn't a father but an absence and whatever brings it
    to your mind,
say, some famous TV father or the dying dad of a friend, or all the old anger
    at your mother
for never talking about the man, that catastrophe of silence, so much
    you'll never know
about her, because she never gave you permission to ask about him—this occurs
    to you as you sit gazing
out your living room window at a flock of geese. The geese arrived this morning,
    hungry, are grazing
on the marshy lawn like sheep. And when one of your neighbors buzzes someone
    into the building
and they all look up at once, talk about unnerving, dozens of little heads
    turning toward you
suddenly, the dark lines of their long necks slicing the air above their squat,
    awkward bodies.
It's one of those moments that makes you wonder what geese are—or trees,
    the crab apples
staining the pavement, the sky's persistent grey. So much you take
    for granted,
this planet, its constant revolution around a ball of fire for goodness sake
    —divine science
or miraculous accident, infinite space brimming with hundreds of millions
    of voices whispering,
Father, where are you? Mama, why won't you talk to me? And then
    a question that ushers
you back to the present, where do geese go when they die? Because there are
    dozens of geese
out there every day, year after year, yet you've never seen a dead goose.
    Do other animals eat them,
carry them off to some secret place? And why now are they running in mass
    toward the river's edge
beating their wings, their wild honks breaking open the day—and your heart,
    a goose.

Semester Abroad

A room in a house just outside of Paris,
no idea I'd be sharing the bath with José, a little Brazilian
who could've passed for one of my cousins, that particular mix
of African, Cherokee and empire. I couldn't understand a word he said,
French poured through a Portuguese accent, plus the landlady
didn't like him, all I needed to justify my annoyance
of the bathroom situation. But weeks in and the landlady *en vacance,*
the power went out, so José lit candles, invited me to share
his pasta with *crème fraiche.* He'd never met his father
either, though his mother's boyfriend bought him art supplies,
paid for drawing classes. I was surprised he was vegetarian,
too, that French was his third language, that I was the provincial.
Nothing happened between us, not even after the bottle of Beaujolais,
not even though I'd been looking for someone to save me
from being bored and lonely in Paris of all places,
only our shadows touching across the walls of that tiny kitchen,
city lights blinking through the foggy window and the realization
that I was no longer translating each word he said, that I understood
him, but even stranger, us—our faces, our very names
the spoils of conquest—our passports and the languages
we spoke and why, our fathers and fathers' fathers, the back story
of millions whittled down to a few pages in high school,
the cowboy and Indian movies my mother refused to stop watching,
that I'd rent for her years later when she was dying,
flying across the Atlantic over the bones of God knows how many Africans
and forgetting to even look down, to remember them if only for a few seconds.
Yes, the unimaginable absence and lack and yet the unknown alive
in that kitchen, too, its contradictions, its silences
and hysterics, the blackness in our voices as we laughed
and talked through the night—a keening, but also a kind of space,
a clearing we could move through.

The Coup

My mother in all her armor
which so rarely came off—her laws, her decrees,
her look that said, *Don't ask me for anything*
before I could ask for anything, that roared
Off with her head! when I asked anyway.
Thus once—in a rare show of defiance—I said,
Then I want to call my father.
And even now I can't believe the words came out of my mouth.
My father, a man my mother had never acknowledged,
whose absence was treated no differently in our house
than, say, not having a cat or washer and dryer.
She looked terrified, like a dictator threatened with a coup,
like a lonely despot betrayed by her most trusted servant,
like a single mother, catching three buses to work,
no idea how she could be the bad guy.

Late Night Science

If reality and existence are debatable,
if I may not be here,
then maybe when I turned from the TV to watch winter
instead I really did go back to Mrs. Newsome's sixth grade class,
maybe she and I really were talking, she hugging me,
me forgiving her for laughing at my big feet,
for taking one look at those aircraft carriers
and confirming, yes, they were huge and everyone could see it.
And thank you Mrs. Newsome for not letting me go through life
fooling myself. You know, like Mississippi, how just hearing the word
is still scary, yet we all say it. My father was from Mississippi,
I got the feet from him even though the last time I saw him I wasn't even walking,
had no idea someday I'd find winter interesting, that I'd grow up to be
the sort of person an ex would catch pretending to be Chaka Khan,
singing my heart out to some imaginary, abstract painter
with a thing for poets. And, oh, Cy Twombly, what wouldn't I do
to know what you thought about Black people and how sad to have to worry
about all my dead crushes' politics, how Larkin ruined everything.
And my father, did I ever thank his son for the photos
he gave me, my brother, yes, though it's hard to know what to call a brother
I met in my thirties. And is existence yet another philosophical theory
I couldn't remember if you put a gun to my head? Was that reality
that showed up after my divorce, constantly making me lose my keys,
dressing me in the same two pairs of pants with different blouses? And then
my new brother found me and suddenly I was wearing make-up again,
planning on the day when I'd take the pictures he gave me out of the Kinkos bag
and put them in the kente cloth photo album that P bought me, yes,
sweet P who'd found his birth mother and thought it was the same thing.
And where *do* my father's pictures fit considering everything
in that dining room cabinet? Should I at least write who he is on the bag
in case something happens—say, I leave behind my long, suffering feet
and become pure spirit, pure me. In case I find myself expanding
across the room, across all of North America—in case I become eternal
and without warning, know that I've always existed and that I always will
—bright light—everything I was going to say, said.

Aubade

Some days I wake up and all I can be is a pair of dark eyes
adjusting to the light behind the curtains, thoughts walking home
with a shoe in each hand. Dear Capitalism, I can't possibly come in today,
but if it makes you feel any better I won't be putting on a bra
either. Instead I'm going to give myself up to a good long stretch,
put my arms under my head and smile like a thief, going to study
that green stripe in the blue scarf on the chair, listen
to the ducks pledge their allegiance to the air. And, oh, books
on the bed, on every table and in every purse,
oh, dull ache and fleeting glimpse of the sublime
in other people's poetry. Are you the reason
I keep forgetting to look for a nice guy? Have a heart,
there's room here for everybody. And please forgive me
Vinyasa yoga class, but sometimes I want to peel off my skin
and go from zero to transcendent all by myself, want to slam
the unknown up against the wall and knock the almighty
out of it, want to shake it and shake it until *yes*
falls out. But not today. Today, I just need to lie here
for as long as I want, the sun tattooing my foot with tiny, tiny dots.

Progress and Reason

Say you and I were Nobel laureates
and we could turn everything we just said
into a vaccine for everything we just said. Say
the science existed and we could cure the tones
of our voices and looks on our faces, wipe out
the coming silent treatment. Yes, rescue dinner,
save this late afternoon walk perfect for talking
about nothing in particular, the poem I'm always
wishing I was writing, the news we're lucky
not to be in. And if I thought we were speaking
I'd point to those wild flowers there by the creek,
wait for you to name them, happy you know things
I don't. Instead, I think about that movie
where Jill Clayburgh takes the painting
and leaves the painter. I see her struggling
down the street carrying it as the music soars,
I think about my mother struggling all her life
sans music. I look around at one blooming thing
after another, the blossoms on your neighbor's crabapple tree
like an infestation of pink cotton candy,
begging us to say something.

Naming Yourself

Lost a few things in all the confusion, modernity's
been hard on people. Friends are already giving lip service

to the question of what to do with their bodies,
you're still stuck on what to call yours, an old scar

you've picked at for as long as you can remember.
You used to think it was out there waiting

for you, the little black dress perfect for every occasion,
the answer to the identity crisis you didn't even know

you were having, your very own box, so many letters down,
so many across—something you could feel good about

putting on a book or passing down to your children
—something to replace the lie passed down to you,

the mess that came with it, yes, shame doing what shame
does for as long as there have been birth certificates,

nations legislating the most natural thing in the world and, oh,
the irony of in relation to the millions displaced or stolen

by those nations—forever living with the consequences
and thus your resolve to find something free of all that misery,

or at least closer to what you'd lost. And how many Amharic,
Yoruba, Hausa, Igbo, Shona, Swahili names—or just cool words—

had you dutifully tried on, none ever quite fitting
the way you wanted, which is to say

without a need for explanation—the pretense
that you'd ever been to Africa. And thus the constant worry

that coming up empty handed might mean you were lost,
too, as if there really was a Lost-and-Found

and you'd simply been too lazy to ask for it.
As if *you* were the one who'd lost it, that if your people

had simply been watching where they were going—as if when Ali
asked a bloody Terrell, *What's my name?* again and again,

he was asking the right person.

Insomnia

When the week has worn you down
to the assorted holes in your head,

all those leased words masquerading
as conversation, all your super powers

used solely for making a living, when all
that's left is the yellow blinking light of your life

half over, nothing to distract you because
it's three in the morning, no denying

the damp sheets and the tangy scent
of your day-old body as your memories

make their crash landing and you cringe
and cower, dreading their arrival. My God,

to be allowed out into the world like that,
a wounded bear disguised as a blue field,

carrying a hurt so old you thought the whole world
limped. When did you discover that knife in your heart

ran in the family, that those were history's long fingers
twisting the handle? And what dumb luck

or good ghost led you from there to here?
Do you dare call it home? Sweet?

TWO

Fall

It took a while for me to ask myself why
my neighbor hung a Christmas wreath
on a door nobody can see except for me.
Just like I never thought to wonder why the leaves
of that big oak we share didn't fall this year.
Sure, I look at the sky, the clouds barely echoes
of clouds, sure I gaze out at a day too warm
for February, the little pillbox houses,
that confused robin. My neighbor
never has company either. Imagine
if instead of leaves, the sky fell, imagine
it happened at the same time each year,
little clumps of blue everywhere
and some people raked it all up into a big pile
and others just left it. Maybe the side door already had a hook
or maybe he put the wreath there for his own enjoyment.
At night it lights up and blinks—no—twinkles.
I fell the other day. It was slippery and I had on heels.
When you fall, no matter how old you are, you want your mother,
you want *somebody* to pick you up and say it's ok.
And if you live alone, there's a particular kind of aloneness
that follows you home afterwards, the kind that seems really unfair,
the kind that makes you sit in the dark staring out the window
and before you know it, you're ripping that wreath to pieces
—not in real life, still there's nothing left when you're finished.
Which you think about the next time you see your neighbor
who's coming toward you—smiling, looking like a nice guy,
no idea of how you set that wreath on fire, danced around it.

Oil Pastels

There are certain days that pull backwards.
I notice it most when I travel, the hours
seeming longer, the present mind conversing

with the past mind. Back home, the world
pulls in other directions and yet the dead
squirrel in the middle of the road,

tiny body looking both ways or the spring trees
like little brown girls showing off their Easter dresses.
Some days I place a piece of paper on the kitchen table

and when the fear I live with shows up,
I put it in there, I put in my guilty solitude,
my lifelong dispute with time, I squeeze

as much gratitude as I can from all my strangeness,
I go in search of the squirrel's bright bounce
and nervous chewing, let the darkness come, too.

Flick

How apt that Hollywood Video is now an urgent care clinic,
still the place to go in the middle of the night if you're broken

or bleeding, the former film student waiting behind the counter
not unlike a doctor on call as you limp from aisle to aisle

unsure of what you're in the mood for, what you want
not there anyway. Remember the year of avoiding couples and happy

endings, Tom Hanks and Meg Ryan killing you softly, and how nice
to no longer have to worry about how it looks to rent so many videos

at one time, that you can savor an entire season of the family
you never had, watch man after man save the day thanks to being a man

and rarely black or brown, which does not stop you from wanting
him to save you, too, as you sit doodling in Monday morning

staff meetings, playing the typical under-employed woman
of African descent, the type who paints large abstract paintings

on her days off, the kind of woman you've never seen in the movies
though you may have a quirky neighbor from Mexico or South Korea,

a bookish type and fellow tree whisperer, the sort of man who could be
the hero in a small indie film, though rarely is, and like would-be heartthrobs

everywhere—has been bathed since birth in all manner of false images
of your people and thus makes certain assumptions which he's desperate

to distance himself from. Yes, a wannabe good guy eager
to un-typecast you, a man who has his own horror stories to tell

and does not accidentally sleep with your sister—no, no concessions
to Hollywood, the script maintaining its complicated view of the world,

steadfast even when he turns out to be married, which does not make him evil
since, O happy day, you did not sleep with him—something told you, yes,

you had a feeling—not that you're some kind of voodoo priestess—sadly,
you have no magical powers—no power at all—beyond this, perhaps, to speak of.

Crash

What she hates is when there's a form
that asks his name, how

without warning,
she's no longer the sleepy driver

of her life, how that one word,
Father,

will muck up the autopilot,
a red light where there wasn't

even a stop sign, a head-on collision
with, of all people, herself, how

even now, knowing his name,
she leaves the space blank.

Roughing It

1.

Each summer we drove north to Lake Michigan,
several couples in our twenties—a week
of walking the dunes and swimming,
of heading out into the dark with a flashlight
and a roll of toilet paper,
a bunch of black people out in the middle of nowhere,
not that we ever talked about that.

2.

They say our memories are actual physical events,
the same neurons firing as during the original experience,
and it's true I can see our tents
in a semi-circle under a canopy of oaks and pines,
hear our quiet conversations in the mornings,
the early risers sipping coffee from the same tin cups
we'd use later to brush our teeth,
our only nod to hygiene, supposedly, besides swimming
though some of us cheated.

And could the nightly camp fires ever be too big,
each of us adding our two cents as the night's storytellers
embellished the day's mishaps, a joint and a bottle
of Peach Schnapps going around and around
until first one couple, then another bid goodnight.

3.

Lately, when the house feels too empty,
I go to the café to write. I like the distractions,
the pretty young woman with two afro puffs
giving a quick peck on the lips
to the girl with blond dreads,
the songs I've never heard
or the songs I haven't heard in years,
Al Green still moaning, *moaning for love,*
that long, high *heeee* that still owns me.

4.

Was I the only one who thought about our parents
during those trips? That generation, witnesses
to every manner of humiliation and threat, how
unlikely it was that they had ever camped,
witnessed the entire spectrum of brown skin
against a blue, sun-speckled lake
in an all white county anywhere in the United States.
Yes, even years after the dark days of assassinations,
of four little girls blown-up in a church, long after my cousins'
grandfather yelled down from the jail that he was already dead,
to take care of his family, days later the undertaker saying
his insides looked like hamburger—was it possible
for the people who lived those stories to truly live?
For my mother, say, to actually enjoy her dinner downtown
each Mother's Day, that tight look on her face,
not that she ever let fear stop her—and, yes, a certain admiration
for that. But also anger. And ask me about the junior high school
she transferred me to, the teachers that refused to call on me,
the students who pretended I wasn't there, that all she said
before giving her shy, awkward child to those people was,
The world is white so you better get used to it.

5.

Late night chill in the air, the books
I'm too sleepy to move shifting
as I pull up the extra blanket, as I recall
how well we all got along, even after a night
of torrential rain, our tents at the bottom of a hill,
even at the end of the week when all
we could think about was a hot shower
and real beds. Huey and Grace, Aaron and Pam,
Michael.

6.

And shouldn't there be a rule
that if you keep a man's name
you have to stay friends?

7.

I don't remember if I ever told my mother
about those trips, only that she and I were still close,
that we talked about everything except the things
we never talked about. No idea if I tried
to convince her, say, of the beauty of a dark wood,
of those impossibly dark nights, black times black
times black draping around us like velvet. Did I ever tell
her about the first time I looked up on a night like that,
the sky so jam packed with stars it was terrifying?

8.

Not that I would've said *terrifying*.

Old song

playing me on this empty house morning
all the window blinds wide open
not one tree not blooming
and the light this time of year
the quality of which the quality of which
as if making it through the day isn't enough
and now you and that voice
asking how long since I doused myself and lit a match
how long since I fueled the God furnace
for desire is and we are
this ceaseless call to temple
a blue physics splitting us atom by blue atom
crazy light that won't go out yes
king queen ruler of everything smashed
and carefully taped back together
see what you've done

Reset

for my cousins, the Davenports and Andersons

When the lack of company starts to get to me, I take a long walk.
 I rub my phone and make a wish, I make a wish

and when I hear the voice I need to hear, when I hear my name,
I walk out of myself toward gratitude, toward my own big smile,

me the black sheep, me the odd bird, I walk out of myself, the world
again a human place, I follow the way of each voice and I talk

and I talk, forgetting my promise, I embarrass myself yet again, oh
but I listen, too, I listen as if Time is calling, as if the next world

is on the other line—I walk, dumbfounded at how few of us are left
to reach through this almost magic, to say *I love you*

before saying goodbye, words once too shy and difficult
to speak—but that lately can hardly wait.

Jump

It seems like years since I had a good laugh or cry
so I go to where I left my heart on the side of the road
and wouldn't you know it's still there. The family
I read about in the paper has the hood up
and that old song, the one with the muddy toes
and plans to change the world, is changing the oil.
I could always use the memory of my grandmother's laugh
to give it a jump, but that would mean recalling how I failed
her so I keep walking. And yet I can sense the story
of that dead family, the kids especially, staring
after me and that sad song isn't happy, insists
I face the music—and what can I do, I go back
and gather up the sweet noise of her, I close my eyes
because the sound is so bright and damning,
especially compared to the life I've been driving like a hearse
and the hunger that's in there pretending to be full. I say,
Grandma, but then I say, *Mama*, because my mouth misses the sound
of both, plus I know otherwise she'll get jealous
and my heart starts right up, revs its little engine
and off we go, still no map to speak of.

Walking Around Kerrytown with K. H.

A portly young man on an old blue Schwinn
with a ring of curly hair
corralling a pale, shaven pate
ding, ding, dinging his bell
before passing on the left,
late summer day divining a cool night,
row after row of clapboard houses
nobody we know can afford
to even rent anymore, my favorite
a small, yellow cottage with faded prayer flags
and an old oak with leaves so green they're black.
You say, *He looks like a whatcha-ma-call-it.*
He yells back, *Friar!*
It's Friday, two whole days ahead
that belong solely to us—already *so much, so much,*
how can we possibly stand it?

Late Spring

It can't all be wild ginger and cherry blossoms,
sometimes there's bound to be a man
standing on a hill above the river
with his young son and yellow dog,
telling the dog to jump, losing his patience
after the second time, the dog looking
from the man to the twist of thrashing water
—run off from the dam, run off from the canal,
water from two directions forced into a small pool,
a long drop, the dog's confusion obvious
from where I'm standing on this favorite trail,
on this wished-for day after weeks of cold and drizzle,
everything in me, until this moment, reaching up,
grateful weed finally free of the dirt.

But it's not all prairie sedge and lilac bushes
a father is a man, not a leaf blade unfurling,
not a patch of skunk cabbage or culver's root.
The boy is maybe six. The man—oblivious
to me, the other walkers, the tall shoots of what looks like poppy,
he takes a step—one step—and the dog jumps.
Is the air holding its breath, is the water? Of course
I keep walking, though perhaps more slowly
and the dog is fine, manages to climb out and shake,
to head up the grassy hill to his master, the man lighting a cigarette
now, staring off. And the boy, his son? The look on his face
never changes, though it's the opposite of a look really,
perhaps as far from a look as a face can get. Not even blank.

Cliché This

When you grow up with a view of the sun setting
over, say, Lake Michigan, are you more susceptible
to what our little star can do under the right circumstances,
are you less dismissive of sunsets on postcards
and calendars than the rest of us, do you grow moody
and out of sorts without your daily hit of miraculous?
Because when I see a great sunset, the sky losing its mind,
sticking a knife in my heart again and again,
I think of that Kenyan oil executive who gave up his millions
to adopt hundreds of street children, I think of his wife
—his sons and daughters who said goodbye to their lives, too,
I think of those kids sleeping in doorways now finishing college.
Yes, with the right sunset—one of those freaky light shows
worthy of its own religion—anything's possible,
if not the man of my dreams, a black lab with a red ball,
his tail running for office. And just think of the first people
who sat where I'm sitting, this beach I had to beg, borrow
and steal to get to, folks who must've thought the waves
were somehow linked to their breathing, who still believed in clouds,
that the world was irreplaceable. And how to watch
this woo-woo of weird light routinely denied to anyone
without vacation time and not swing wide my arms
as if I'm not the only black person out here, how to stand up
and shake out my towel as if all that star shine
isn't still rearranging my soft machinery, crashing me,
handing me back like an invitation.

If my father could talk

he'd claim I made a deal with the moon
to keep him up nights, insist that when he started the chemo
and stopped drinking, I reached into his chest and squeezed
just for the fun of it. I'd tell him that line about the moon
is cliché and that even for a ghost he's being melodramatic.
Of course, he can explain everything—Ms. Truth,
John Brown, Fannie Lou Hamer—all the great minds
at his disposal now, not to mention his father
and his father's father, each shy as a toddler the first time
they meet each other. He won't say when he decided to come clean
with his family, when he realized he still had something I needed
—the photos, that video from the family picnic.
He's totally OK with me putting words into his mouth,
by the way, says by all means dump him into a big pot
with a spoon so the whole world can eat. Suggests
that when folks are full, I take the scraps and turn
him into a space ship, says I'm wrong about the moon,
it always has something new to say.

THREE

There are signs everywhere,

the looks my mother used to give me alive
and well on my face, my ear itching, all morning
the feeling there's something I'm forgetting,
the house on Spring Street coming to my mind
for no reason, the high ceilings, the wood floors
tragically painted and chipping, the self-portraits
by the man I lived with on every wall, fighting
with the free sofa, the man I loved whose paintings
I merely liked. Yes, those days of potlucks and friends
from every other continent, Teresa
moving in for a few weeks and staying a year,
the three of us, our Sundays together sharing
the paper, two of us with no idea it was stolen
from our neighbors. And how to reconcile
my former lover's pathological propensities
with all the fun we had, his homemade crepes?
And that tonight, of all nights, Teresa calls,
that she's walking home from a party
where she was hoping to meet someone, her fate
instead to find a copy of *Pudd'nhead Wilson* and read
it from cover to cover, to sit tucked in a corner
drinking as much of the Merlot as she wanted,
to insist later when I answer the phone
that Mark Twain is a hottie and when I'm not convinced,
to ask if I've ever seen him shirtless.

Settling

Divorced more years than married, I look down
at the name in my wallet, the so-called placeholder
and think, *Why not just be her and be done with it?*
A lover of Honey Crisp apples and curly kale,
single parent to an indestructible weeping fig
and a series of small collages lounging around my apartment
like surly teenagers, each one a disappointment. Yes, why not
just another walker meandering towards town, following
the river with the hope that the peony garden
is in full swing by now, which is how I meet that family
of red buds on the edge of the little park, screaming
hot pink, making a scene, nailing me on the head
without so much as an introduction.

To Milwaukee

People are always surprised at how clean you are.
Remember when I was almost hit by that car?
Every time I see this red clay, I think about your black dirt.
I think about kindergarten and the 4th Street Projects,
the bald lawns and cinderblock walls,
the mentally challenged man on the stairs
after school with his thing in his hand,
how I said *Excuse me* before stepping around him.
This morning, as I walk the river, I think about my mother
with her year of college, changing bedpans
at the County to get us out of there.
Thus the flat on 7th, the flat on 12th, the flat on 16th,
all before I understood what cereal for dinner meant,
the jar of leftover soap under the sink, those days of bible stories
—David, Joseph and Daniel—not one of them praying
for their breasts to stop growing, for what to do about the boy
sent down like a plague and yet that lucky kick, the principal
saying I could've killed him, deciding then to be a killer.

Today, climbing these muddy hills, I see me and my mother
riding the bus to Germantown, the sweet smell of hops
turning bitter and sharp, I see our bags full
of hog-head cheese and liverwurst, bratwurst
and warm potato salad. And thank you buses for running
on time, thank you A. O. Smith for giving all the men in our family jobs,
thank you white people for disappearing overnight, terrified,
leaving those sturdy brick houses on both sides of Capital Drive,
all the elm trees and parks happy to stay with us, the streets
wide enough for kickball and go-carts, streets it's true
I walked unsmiling, a question I couldn't ask following me.

A river runs through you Milwaukee and a bar sits on every other corner,
but the Atkinson Street Library was my altar, my house of worship.
Not that I regret one choir practice, Calvary Baptist,
your hallelujahs, your Lord-have-mercies my first language. I want
to go home with my Cousin Vish after service and watch
the boys and their father leave their bodies as the ball falls
in the right hands, I want to wrap myself in their rooster and gander,

want them to ask me if I'm hungry and make me a sandwich.
Because forget what you've heard: there are no unarmed black men,
only sons who vacuum and get dinner started, only brothers
who join the marines and come home in their right minds,
only neighbors, that cutie pie around the corner, somebody's first
boyfriend. And where are you Tommy Harris?
Aren't we glad my mother stuck her head in that living room
so often? Let's go to the lake like it's a hot night
and half the city is already there, let's sit on your hood
without saying one word about who we are and what we want.

And who am I, Lake Michigan—my little ocean, my great lake?
Who else drives all that way each year and only puts her feet in?
Today I read that the city where we met might mean *gathering place
by the water*, might be Potawatomi or Ojibwe—Milwaukee,
ground that holds my mother, that I hope to be sprinkled on,
tell me your story and I'll tell you mine.

Game Day

Pretty one-legged woman coming down Shamrock,
that small mountain calling itself a hill,
elegant grasshopper,
unlikely kamikaze,
daredevil minus one ski,
everything about you is wrong with this picture—
your polite hair, your clothes quietly confessing money,
your crutches that are not wings.
What were you thinking?
My car can barely get up this behemoth,
this prima donna, my way home,
love rollercoaster I will never walk up or down
again without thinking of you.
I see you standing there at the top, little bird
pondering your options and I say, *Please don't,*
I say, *Oh honey. . . oh lady,*
yes, oh, me of little faith
imagining the too, too terrible,
the black top of the street a small galaxy
between us, the afternoon deserted
except for the distant roar of the game day crowd
that's cheering even now.

There

I'll be there . . .
        The Jackson Five

I'll take you there . . .
        The Staple Singers

I may not get there with you . . .
        Martin Luther King, Jr.

Will it be bathed in blue light, a room with a view
and stars for days? Or is that too predictable?
How about the outer limits of what we're made of,
everything stretched to blessed—our dreams, our intuitions
all those funny feelings and so-called coincidences
verified, illuminated. Or some other dimension
turning like a page whenever the clock strikes
our secret hour, that round sound taking us back
to blue. Or will Time finally be free
of us, can dark and light be themselves, the world
complicated? Our hearts filling up and spilling over
because that's what they were made to do,
our minds wondering who's wondering,
pressed to the window of everything. And yet
maybe *there* isn't that different from *here,* maybe
we need to take off the divine handcuffs,
go dancing, say, at the Elks Club, Aretha singing,
You make me feel, you make me feel . . . ,
the whole world finishing her sentence.
Maybe we need to stand closer to the edge, jump
without thinking—fall, yes, *fall*
resplendent in our own bad planning.
Or will we find it only when there's no jump left
in us, when we're lost and all alone,
no hope, no possibility of reprieve,
still somehow we get out of bed,
put on a little lipstick just in case.

The Hero Chiwara

—sculpture of a female antelope and calf
  from the Bamana People of Mali in the Fralin Art Museum

Things fall apart, but they won't let me.
My hoo-doo all gone—what could survive
these white walls—and yet this wood and straw
are worth twice the guard's salary.
As if I'm anything without a head to sit on,
seeds to bless, entire farming communities
believing in me. It's true, our aesthetic traditions
are so far-reaching the so-called West
had to rethink Beauty (*Greek this, Greek that*)
and yet before I could say conquest,
I was sitting here no different than that big square
of dripping paint. Not that I have a problem
with abstraction—ask Picasso, my boy Matisse.
But where are my harvests, my markets full of millet,
rice and sweet potatoes? This place doesn't even have seasons,
no ritual, no dancing in unison, only these polite gatherings,
signs that say *No Touching.* Yet today a familiar face,
last month there were three. *Come closer*, I whisper,
try to say my name.

TV Fathers

Bill Cosby was never my fantasy father
but he was my girlfriend Debbie's,
even before the Huxtables,
even though she already had a father,
back when Cosby was still driving a go-cart
on his comedy albums, pretending to be Fat Albert and The Gang,
which we could listen to because he never said bad words
or talked about sex unless it was over our heads.
No, for me it was Lorne Greene and his oldest son Adam on *Bonanza*,
all the brothers on *Big Valley*, the sidekick on the *Wild Wild West*
and once, long after I should've grown out of the habit,
there was Lucky Luciano.
I don't remember the name of the show or the actor,
but like Don Corleone he wasn't your typical mob boss,
it was about circumstances, his character perennially sad
for the life he could have had, a man who wanted to be a river
but for the sake of La Famiglia had to be a mirror
or a glass of water. And do you think I cared that in real life
he was a murderer and a pimp? Even now my mind misses the theater
of us—him tucking me into bed, amazed at my deep kid questions,
arriving just in time to watch me make the winning basket—
yes, all my favorite TV daddy moments starring *me, me, me!*
And please don't ask why Lucky Luciano,
please don't look for the logic or the sense, just know
that when I needed someone to lift me up
and show me off to the moon,
he was there.

Dear Saturday

don't change a hair for me,
outrageous clouds,
I want to hold your hand, I want joy
to be little bells on my shoes—love
homemade pound cake, my mother alive
and having seconds. Sometimes when my friend Maria smiles,
she gets a little dimple and science has no idea why,
she gets a little dimple and only our hearts can explain
it. Dear just-cut grass, if you know where this poem is going,
please point me in the right direction, take me to the bridge
and shake me like a rug over my neighbor's black-eyed Susans,
let me be that person walking down the street smiling
for no reason, let whoever sees me smile, too,
don't just hint at the truth, tell me why
some men I know never smile for the camera,
why sliced watermelon isn't just fruit.
And, oh, sweetgum tree, your name makes me so happy,
why can't we all be like you, your wide, patient trunk,
your kind leaves that have their reasons, that somehow know
that though my mind is a muddy pond, these words
can turn water into air, their bright bodies gladly disturbing the dark.

This poem is not about Facebook

—for the 2017 Women's March

or me posing in front of the ocean with my girls
from undergrad in our royal blue dresses,
none of my other friends imagining me in a sorority,
surprised at how large I am, my contradictions.
And O cousins I haven't seen in years,
O poets like family, O friend
of a friend wishing your *Peaches* a happy birthday,
praising Jesus, praying for the Greenbay Packers,
I scroll down you, I look for the end of the page.
I voyage through this vast, mixed up, overflowing,
puffed up, brilliant, confused, too happy nation,
all the roads, mountains, weddings and camel rides
familiar, an all you can eat buffet. It's fifty degrees
in January in Ann Arbor, Michigan and I'm wondering why
we're not afraid, why some people can walk on the moon
and never leave home while others are born waving the wrong flag.
I'm staring at a day without car bombs, without a father
putting his child back together like a jigsaw puzzle,
yet I see my black skin and those blue dresses against the Atlantic
and I make the connection, I remember what I should never forget. O kin
of everything packed inside this fat, shiny now,
this morning I sit in a noisy café where there are no whites-only signs,
where young sisters of every kind of fabulous are studying
to be what their mothers couldn't, I touch a line of blue text
and without so much as an abracadabra
I watch millions marching like it's 1963—none of it magic.

Aubade With Sugar Maple

When the hard edges of the book
that sang me to sleep, woke me
I assumed thoughts of all I hadn't accomplished
weren't far behind, the people I'd disappointed,
the money I hadn't made,
the power structure I'd rarely opposed.
But instead I found myself greeted
by an almost criminal hope, somehow free
of the social order that had shaped
my mind so that by the time the sun peeked in
and the huge sugar maple that filled my window
spoke, the only thing I questioned
was the forty hour work week, why the French
and Italians got *eight* weeks vacation.
Because it's been what—a million years?
And yet somehow that maple knew me. We talked
and talked until I became birched and oaked,
crabappled and cherried—drunk
with all the tree-ness I'd forgotten.
My God, to think—I could bud, even blossom.

In the Future

we'll be able to say *I'm lonely*
without sounding pathetic, we'll be able to walk up
to a complete stranger and say, *Please hold me. Tighter,*
we can say, *Tighter.* I can say I miss my family, holidays
at Terry's, how the air felt like it was filled with confetti,
a ticker-tape parade in every room, the laughter, the stories
—the world small, packed with people who loved
me, the din of their voices filling my body
and where did it go?

And when my mother gets sick in the future
and I move her and her mother
into my two-bedroom condo,
I'll be the daughter I thought I could be,
my family like a family
in the movies, not the one where the sister
pushes the other sister down the stairs,
perhaps a space movie, space before Time
or History, before cancer or Alzheimer's,
before there was even a planet,
the three of us just spheres of plasma
held together by gravity—*luminous,*
no idea that we're stars.

And the world? Will it be safer
in the future, the rapists and pillagers dead
tired, weary to the bone, money no longer the answer
to our problems—greed out, people in—
everybody walking, riding their bikes, slowly
forgetting the thrill of catching all the lights.

Of course, we'll still have our differences,
the void inside us still bottomless,
but thanks to those public service announcements
we'll know that rusty can rubbing against our hearts
is standard issue. Thus, when the man in my future
heads to his workroom one night,
when he starts hammering and drilling,

desperate to fix what's broken
inside, I'll climb into bed and when he's had enough
and thinks he just wants to sleep,
I'll turn off the light, I'll change his mind.

Story of My Life

And yet this bright spur
inside of me—specter and marrow,

waves and waves of vanishing light,
so much pulling at me and through me,

that I'll need to find a quiet place
and spread it all out.

NOTES

"Milwaukee, 1968"
"Say It Loud—I'm Black and I'm Proud" is a song performed by James Brown and written with his bandleader Alfred "Pee Wee" Ellis in 1968.

"Late Night Science"
Cy Twombly was an American painter, sculptor and photographer.

Philip Larkin was a highly regarded English poet whose letters, which were published in 1992, include a number of racist statements.

"Progress and Reason"
Jill Clayburgh was known for her role in the film *An Unmarried Woman*, for which she was nominated for an Academy Award.

"Naming Yourself"
Muhammad Ali vs. Ernie Terrell was a professional boxing match fought in 1967, which Ali won through a unanimous decision. It was the first fight that Ali fought after changing his name from Cassius Clay. Before the fight, Terrell taunted Ali by referring to him by his former name. During the bout, Ali punched Terrell repeatedly while asking him, "What's my name?"

"If my father could talk"
Ms. Truth refers to Sojourner Truth, an abolitionist and women's rights activist, who was born into slavery and escaped with her infant daughter.

John Brown was an American abolitionist who believed in and advocated armed insurrection as the only way to overthrow the institution of slavery in the United States.

Fannie Lou Hamer was an American voting and women's rights activist, community organizer, and a leader in the civil rights movement.

"Game Day"
"Love Rollercoaster" is a funk/R&B song by the Ohio Players, originally featured on their 1975 album *Honey*.

ACKNOWLEDGMENTS

I'm grateful to the editors of the following publications in which some of the poems have appeared or are forthcoming: *TriQuarterly*; *Foundry*; *Black Renaissance Noire*; *St. Petersburg Review*; *Kweli*; *Serendipity*; *The Cortland Review*; *Mead Magazine*; *Clover Literary Rag*; and *Furious Flower: Seeding the Future of African American Poetry*.

Grateful acknowledgment to the following institutions: the University of Virginia Creative Writing Program; Cave Canem; The Furious Flower Poetry Center; The University of Michigan Afroamerican and African Studies Department; Bennington College; The Vermont College of Fine Arts; the Hocking Hills Festival of Poetry.

My sincere gratitude to the following early supporters of my work: Major Jackson, Ed Ochester, Patricia Smith, Jack Ridl and Franc Nunoo-Quarcoo.

Big love and gratitude to my University of Virginia family for all their time and support: Greg Orr, Jeffery Renard Allen , Rita Dove, Paul Guest, Debra Nystrom, Lisa Russ Spaar, Sara Brickman, Michael Dhyne, Quinn Gilman Forlini, Landis Grenville, Nichole LeFebvre, Michaela Cowgill, Bobby Elliott, Sasha Prevost, Sean Shearer, Anna Tomlinson, Rob Shapiro, Caitlin Neely, Annie Pittman, Veronica Kuhn, Courtney Flerlage and Teresa Kim.

And heartfelt thanks to my friends: Roz, Charnita, Patrice, Jan, Madeline, Kathe, Alesia, Andrea, Paul, Maria, Fanny, Jia and Lindsay.

And finally thank you to everyone at Persea Books and the Lexi Rudnitsky Poetry Project, most notably Gabe Fried for his editorial diligence and insight.